Der EY! – Laut
im Englischen
mit Simple Presen

Jake Snake

Jake Snake

Hey du!

- siehst du a-e wie in snake

- ay wie in play

- ai wie in paint

- ea wie in great

liest du beide Buchstaben als

EY

Das hört sich so an, als würdest du „EY Alter" oder „Boah EY!" sagen.

This is a snake.

His name is Jake.

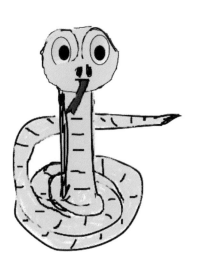

Jake has got
a lake.
It is Jake's lake.

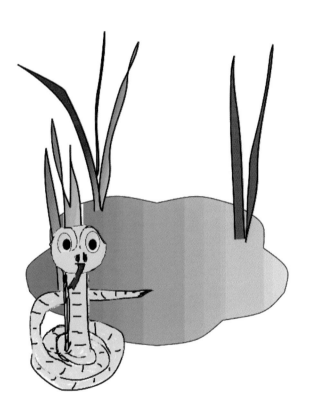

Jake plays in his lake.

It is a lake for Jake.

It is Jake's lake.

Jake plays in
his lake all day.
He can't go away.
He must stay.

He has to stay in his cage all day, but that is okay.

Jake paints in
his cage.
He can paint with
his tail.
That is great!

Jake can make
a sail
with his tail.

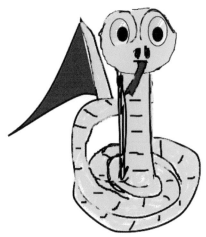

He sails in
his lake.

Then Jake
takes a break.

Say...
is that Jake's
best mate?

Great!
Jake has a full
plate!

Too late!

Im Deutschen EY! – im Englischen:

a -e	ay	ea	ai
snake	play	great	paint
name	day	break	tail
Jake	away		sail
lake	say		
cage	okay		
mate	stay		
late			

Im Deutschen EY! – im Englischen:

a -e	ay	ea	ai
make			
take			
plate			

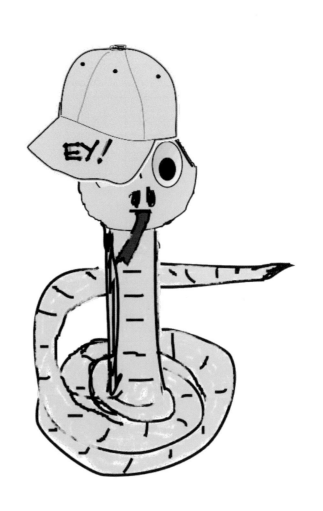

Printed in Great Britain
by Amazon